# SALSAS AND TACOS

# SALSAS AND TACOS

## Santa Fe School of Cooking

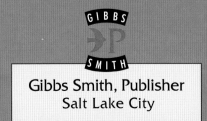

Gibbs Smith, Publisher
Salt Lake City

First Edition
16 15            16

Published by
Gibbs Smith, Publisher
P.O. Box 667
Layton, Utah 84041

Orders: 1.800.748.5439
www.gibbs-smith.com

Interior Designed by Forthgear
Printed and bound in China

Library of Congress Control Number: 2005935849

ISBN-10: 1-4236-0015-0
ISBN-13: 978-1-4236-0015-2

This cookbook is dedicated to the friends and guests of the
Santa Fe School of Cooking, whose loyal support and patronage
helped the school achieve success beyond anyone's wildest dreams.

# ✺ CONTENTS ✺

# SALSAS & TACOS MAKE THE FIESTA

Top chefs from The Santa Fe School of Cooking have filled this book with the tastiest recipes taken from a popular little book titled *Salsas* and another wildly admired tiny book titled *Tacos*. Here the best and boldest recipes come together to offer the most satisfying combinations of genuine southwestern cooking. We have included full-colored photographs, step-by-step instructions, resources for ingredients, and cooking techniques and equipment that you will need to prepare your very own flavorful, unforgettable fiesta.

It's an unwritten rule that anytime you serve tacos, you must also serve salsa. One spectacular salsa or many varied salsas, the number doesn't matter—only the taste. *Salsa*, the Spanish word for "sauce," can be fresh (raw) or cooked, thick or thin, chunky or smooth, crunchy, hot, spicy, mild, sweet, savory, tart, etc. Salsas can be used as a side dish, condiment or relish, as an ingredient in other dishes, or even with a dessert. They can be made from vegetables, fruits, or a combination of both, and are usually served at room temperature but are sometimes chilled.

Many of the salsas have chiles in them. The recipes are rated: 1 chile=mild *(suave)*, 2 chiles=medium *(picante)*, and 3 chiles=hot *(muy picante)*. Add chile according to your taste and to suit your guests. It's best to offer mild and hot so everyone has a choice. Remember, the heat of each kind of chile may vary, so take a small taste before adding. For example, fresh jalapeños are generally considered hot: however, in some instances, they can be quite mild. Thus, adapt the recipe to the heat of the chiles you use. If you want no heat, omit the chiles.

Testing the recipes for this book was a catalyst for many festive parties. Whereas wine-tasting parties tend to be on the stuffy side, salsa and taco tasting fiestas bring out the revelry in guests. From Santa Fe's charming adobes to rooftops in the nation's capital, parties have been hosted so guests could sample, critique, and enjoy the recipes in this book. Try it yourself. Mix up some margaritas, make some tacos, grill some meat, and supply a lot of chips to go with these salsas—now you're on your way to a spirited party.

# INGREDIENTS FOR SALSAS

**Avocado** — Oval-shaped fruit with a greenish, buttery-tasting flesh. The Hass avocado, with its bumpy brownish-black skin, is the preferred variety for taste. To ripen, leave at room temperature for a day or two, or place in a paper bag to hasten.

**Chicos** — Corn that has been partially shucked, roasted on the cob, dried, and removed from the cob. The result is a chewy but flavorful kernel requiring a long cooking time.

**Cilantro** — Fresh plant from the coriander seed; however, it is not interchangeable with the seed. It is a delicate, aromatic herb of the parsley family. To store, recut the stem ends and place in shallow water. Cover with a plastic bag and store in the refrigerator. Readily available in most grocery stores.

**Epazote** — A pungent herb that grows wild in Mexico and the United States. It is used frequently in seasoning beans and also acts as an anti-flatulent for beans.

**Huitlacoche**, or **cuitlacoche** — A silvery-grey to black fungus, commonly known as smut in the United States, that is cultivated in the kernels of corn. The puffy kernels, or lobes, can be detached from the ears and kept refrigerated for several days. It is usually found frozen or canned and is considered a delicacy in Mexico.

**Jicama** — A tan-skinned tuber. The flavor of the crisp white flesh is compared to that of a water chestnut or a sweet radish. Primarily used uncooked.

**Mexican Oregano** — A weedy-flavored herb reminiscent of, but distinctly different from, the more common Mediterranean oregano. It is used in the dry whole-leaf form vs. the ground form.

**Mexican Vanilla Bean** — The pod of a tropical orchid vine. It is native to the New World, dating back to the Aztec culture.

**New Mexican** or **Southwestern Piñon Nuts** — Similar to imported pine nuts but much richer in flavor and oil. They should be stored in the freezer to preserve freshness.

**Nopales** — Cactus paddles or the paddle-shaped stems from several varieties of the prickly pear cactus plants. The flavor is somewhat similar to a green bean. They are commonly used in Mexican and southwestern cooking.

**Posole** — Dried corn that has been boiled in a hydrate-lime solution to remove the husk, resulting in an increase in the nutrient value. Used extensively in the Southwest as a side dish or soup.

**Tomatillo** — A tart green fruit used frequently in Mexican sauces. In appearance only, it resembles a small green tomato in papery husks. It is a close relative of the cape gooseberry that grows wild in the United States. Fresh tomatillos are available in most grocery stores.

# ROASTING AND TOASTING CHILES

**Fresh Chiles and Bell Peppers** — Fresh chiles and bell peppers are roasted to intensify their flavor, impart smokiness, and facilitate removing the skin.

Our favorite method is to roast chiles and peppers over a burner using the Santa Fe Grill or over a hot fire on a charcoal grill. Chiles may also be roasted under the broiler of a conventional oven.

Arrange chiles so that they are as close to the heat source as possible and keep watch over them. Using tongs, turn them several times as they begin to blister and darken to ensure even charring of the skin.

When 80 to 90 percent of the skin is blistered or blackened, place chiles in a paper or plastic bag or in a bowl covered with plastic wrap and steam for 10 to 15 minutes. Gently peel the charred skin from the chile; a few bits of remaining skin lend a rustic quality to the chile and are not a problem.

*Caution:* You may want to wear rubber or plastic gloves to protect your hands from the chile oils that can cause skin irritation. Also, do not touch your face, eyes or nose when handling chiles until after you have thoroughly washed your hands in soap and water.

**Dried Whole Chiles** — Arrange the chiles in a layer on a preheated 300- to 325-degree heavy skillet or cast-iron comal. You may also use a baking sheet in a 325-degree oven. Toast the whole chiles, turning several times, until they have softened and begin to darken around the edges (about 2 to 3 minutes). Remove from heat.

When cool, remove the stem, seeds, and seed membranes. Discard these. Then, proceed with chiles as directed in the recipe.

**Spices, Herbs, Seeds, and Ground Chile** — Dry toasting is a method used to intensify the flavors of dry ingredients. In a dry, medium-hot, heavy skillet or comal, toast the ingredients one at a time, stirring or shaking the pan to prevent burning. When the color has begun to deepen and little wisps of smoke start to form, remove immediately and let cool.

Whole seeds may be ground to powder in a coffee grinder or with a mortar and pestle (called a molcajete in Spanish). Toast only what is needed for a particular recipe as most ingredients do not keep well after the application of heat.

**Tomatoes and Tomatillos** — To roast tomatoes and tomatillos, arrange them on a Santa Fe Grill, a hot comal, or under a broiler. Turn them several times for even roasting, until most of the skin has been charred. Place in a bowl to save the juices. Carefully remove the charred skins. The tomato and tomatillo flesh may be pureed or chopped for sauces and salsas.

# ⚲ CHILES ⚲

Different chiles vary widely in their flavor, spice and heat. The definition of the English word *piquancy* is "a spiciness, zest, tang or nip." The Spanish word *picante* means "sharp, hot and spicy to the taste." Below we provide an estimated piquancy level, or an informal heat gauge, for chiles used in Favorite Salsas and Tacos recipes. But, remember, the cook is the best judge. Taste a bit of the chile you plan to use in a recipe before you add it so that your tongue can measure for itself the interplay of flavor, spice and heat that particular chile provides. Then, add just enough according to your desire.

**Ancho** — A wrinkled-skinned, heart-shaped dark cranberry red chile, the ancho is the dried form of the ripened fresh poblano chile. The chile has sweet, dried fruit flavors reminiscent of prunes, raisins, figs, coffee, and tobacco. Mild to medium piquancy level.

**Anaheim** — Sometimes sold as California green, this hybrid form of the New Mexico green chile is a milder and slightly larger pepper with a light green color. Mild piquancy level.

**Chile de Arbol** — A small, hot and flavorful, bright red chile related to the cayenne. Hot piquancy level.

**Chile Caribe** — This is the crushed form of the dried New Mexico red chile. Medium piquancy level.

**Chipotle** — The smoked and dried version of the fresh jalapeño chile or pepper, the Chipotle is dusty brown and ridged with a wrinkled skin. This chile has a rich, smoky, tobacco-like flavor with an intense heat. Very hot piquancy level.

**Chipotle Chiles in Adobo Sauce** — Chipotle chiles pickled in a sauce consisting primarily of tomatoes, vinegar, garlic, onion and other Mexican spices. Sold in whole chile and pureed forms. Slightly less heat than the whole dry chipotle. Hot piquancy level.

**Guajillo** — This dried red chile pod looks similar to the New Mexico red chile but is actually smaller and somewhat darker in color with an earthy, slightly bitter flavor. Medium piquancy level.

**Habanero** — An extremely hot yet full-flavored lantern-shaped chile used extensively in the Yucatan. Freezes easily without changing flavor or texture. Ranging in color from lime green to bright orange, this chile is known for its aroma of tropical fruits and flowers as well as for its heat. Caribbean varieties are often called Scotch Bonnet peppers. Extremely hot piquancy level.

(continued on next page)

(continued from previous page)

**Jalapeño** — This small, fresh dark green chile with a thick flesh is usually fairly hot, but milder varieties are increasingly available. Usually the smaller and darker the jalapeño, the hotter it is. The jalapeño is the most widely recognized hot green chile. Used fresh in most Mexican foods, the chiles are also popular as a condiment pickled with carrots or sliced as a topping over nacho chips. Mild to hot piquancy level.

**Morita** — Another dried and smoked jalapeño chile but more reddish in color than the chipotle. Hot piquancy level.

**New Mexico Green Chiles** — This fresh green chile, about 4 to 6 inches in length, has three primary varieties that range from mild to hot. Usually roasted and peeled, they are stuffed with cheese for chile rellenos or chopped for sauces and stews. Medium piquancy level.

**New Mexico Red Chiles** — The green chile has been vine-ripened until it turns red, and is then dried. These chiles have a bright, fruity flavor and are often tied together to form a decorative ristra for storage. They are available as whole pods, crushed (caribe), or ground into a fine powder. Piquancy level varies from mild to hot.

**Poblano** — A wide-shouldered, thick-fleshed, dark green chile usually roasted and peeled to bring out its full flavor. The poblano is used for chile rellenos, sauces, and salsas. Mild to medium piquancy level.

**Serrano** — A small, cylindrical, fresh dark green chile is similar to the jalapeño but smaller and thinner. The serrano can be interchanged with the jalapeño but has a hotter flavor. Hot piquancy level.

# GRILLED NOPAL AND POBLANO CHILE SALSA

David Jones, a former instructor at the Santa Fe School of Cooking, experienced this relish in Mexico. He recommends it as a side dish or a garnish for tacos, carne adovada, or grilled meats. South of the border, nopales are plentiful as well as economical.

*Yield: about 1-1/2 cups*

**2 prickly pear cactus paddles (nopales), about 7 to 8 ounces**

**2 tablespoons vegetable oil**

**1 red bell pepper**

**2 poblano chiles, about 5 to 6 ounces**

**1/4 cup diced red onion**

**1 teaspoon minced garlic**

**1/4 cup chopped fresh cilantro**

**3 to 4 tablespoons extra virgin olive oil**

**2 to 3 tablespoons sherry vinegar**

**1/2 teaspoon freshly ground cumin**

**Coarse salt to taste**

(continued on next page)

# GRILLED NOPAL AND POBLANO CHILE SALSA

(continued from previous page)

1. Lay a cactus paddle on a flat surface and run the blade of a sharp knife around the outside edge of the paddle from the narrow end toward the large rounded end and back down again, cutting off the cactus spines around the edges in the process. Then, slice the spines from the surface of the paddle one at a time with the tip of a sharp paring knife. Rinse the paddle and pat dry with paper towels. Repeat the process with the remaining paddle.

2. Brush the cleaned paddles with vegetable oil and sprinkle with salt. Grill over a direct flame until the skin is blackened in spots and the cactus paddle has softened slightly. Set aside to cool. Cut the cactus into quarter-inch dice. Set aside.

3. Grill the red pepper and poblano chiles and place them in a plastic bag to cool. Remove the skin, stem, and seeds from the pepper and chiles and cut them into quarter-inch dice. Mix the nopales, the pepper, and the chiles with the remaining ingredients in a bowl; let stand for 20 minutes before serving.

# TROPICAL FRUIT SALSA

This summer salsa is a contribution from Peter Zimmer, one of our most creative chefs. Its flavors complement fish and seafood, but it would also pair well with grilled poultry, lamb, or barbecued game.

*Yield: about 3 cups*

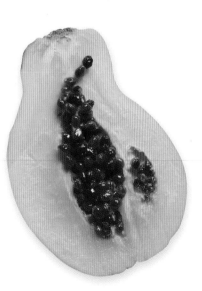

1/2 ripe papaya, peeled, seeded, and cut into quarter-inch dice

1/4 ripe pineapple, peeled, cored, and cut into quarter-inch dice

1 ripe mango, peeled, seeded, and cut into quarter-inch dice

3 fresh black figs, cut vertically into sixths (dried figs may be substituted if fresh are not available)

1 small red onion, peeled, cut into half-inch slices, charred over a flame, then chopped

1 red bell pepper, trimmed and cut into thin strips

Juice and minced zest of 1 lime

Juice and minced zest of 1 lemon

Juice and minced zest of 1 orange

1 tablespoon finely chopped fresh mint

1 tablespoon finely chopped fresh cilantro

2 to 3 teaspoons peeled and minced fresh ginger

1 tablespoon rice wine vinegar

1 tablespoon lime- or orange-flavored olive oil

Pinch of salt

Pinch of sugar to taste

1. Combine all ingredients and season to taste. Set aside for 20 minutes while flavors meld. Serve at room temperature or chilled.

*Tip: This works well as a base for ceviche. Fold the diced uncooked fish into the salsa and marinate for 24 hours in the refrigerator. The citrus chemically "cooks" the seafood.*

# HUITLACOCHE-ROASTED CORN RELISH

The flavors of a simple roasted chicken or filet of beef would be greatly enhanced by this rustic, flavorful addition. Don't let the exotic ingredient (huitlacoche) keep you from trying this fabulous recipe.

*Yield: about 2-1/2 cups*

**3 ears of corn**
**2 tablespoons canola oil**
**1/2 cup diced white onion**
**2 garlic cloves, roasted,**
    **very finely chopped**
**1 cup red wine**
**1/2 cup (4 oz.) canned or**
    **frozen huitlacoche**

**1 tablespoon juice from chipotle**
    **chiles in adobo sauce,**
    **or 1 tablespoon pureed chipotle**
    **chiles in adobo sauce**
**2 teaspoons fresh epazote,**
    **or 1 teaspoon dried epazote**
**1/4 cup cilantro chiffonade**
**Coarse salt and freshly ground**
    **black pepper to taste**

1. Shuck the ears of corn and remove the silk. Roast the ears over direct flame, turning frequently, until blackened in places. Set aside. When the ears have cooled, cut the kernels from the cob and place them in a bowl. There should be about 1-1/2 cups.

2. Heat the canola oil in a skillet over medium heat. Add the onion and saute until golden, 4 to 5 minutes. Add the roasted garlic and red wine; reduce by half. Add the huitlacoche, chipotle chiles in adobo sauce, and epazote. Continue to cook over low heat, stirring frequently, for 8 to 10 minutes, until most of the liquid has evaporated. Remove from the heat and cool.

3. Add the roasted corn kernels and the cilantro to the "dry" mixture and stir to combine well. Season to taste with salt and pepper and serve at room temperature.

# ROASTED TOMATILLO SALSA

This is one of many salsa recipes developed by Chef Kathi Long. In addition to being an instructor at the Santa Fe School of Cooking, she is a personal chef, restaurant consultant, and cookbook author. Kathi recommends this deeply flavored, rustic-looking tomatillo salsa as the ultimate sauce for cheese or chicken enchiladas. It is probably the favorite green salsa at the school.

*Yield: 2-1/2 cups*

**1 pound tomatillos (about 10 to 12 medium), soaked, husked, and dried**

**2 to 3 fresh serrano chiles, stemmed**

**1 small white onion, peeled, cut into half-inch-thick slices, and separated into rings**

**2 to 3 garlic cloves, peeled**

**2 tablespoons olive oil**

**Coarse salt and freshly ground black pepper to taste**

**1/3 cup water**

**1/4 cup coarsely chopped fresh cilantro**

**Pinch of sugar to taste (optional)**

1. Preheat the oven to 475 degrees. Position the rack on the second-highest level from the top of the oven. Place the tomatillos, serranos, onion rings, and garlic cloves in a bowl and toss with olive oil and a sprinkling of salt and coarsely ground black pepper. Pour the ingredients onto a foil-lined baking sheet, distribute evenly, and roast for 10 to 12 minutes, until the ingredients are soft and lightly browned. Remove from the oven and cool.

2. Coarsely chop the serranos, onion, and garlic by hand and place in a medium bowl. Pulse the tomatillos with their juice to a coarse puree in the food processor, then add to the bowl with the chile-onion-garlic mixture. Add the water and stir in the cilantro. Taste and adjust seasonings, adding a pinch of sugar if needed. Serve.

# ROASTED CORN AND ANASAZI BEAN SALSA

James Campbell Caruso is the originator of this salsa that relies on the staples of southwestern cuisine—beans, corn, and chile. He grew up in a household of professional chefs, bakers, and exceptional home cooks. James has been teaching at the Santa Fe School of Cooking since 1998 and is the executive chef at El Farol, a popular Spanish tapas restaurant in Santa Fe. He recommends serving this corn-and-bean salsa with grilled meat or as a side to tamales.

*Yield: 3 cups*

**2 ears of corn, husked**
**1-1/2 cups Anasazi beans, cooked, rinsed, and drained**
**2 jalapeño chiles, seeded and diced**
**2 tablespoons chopped fresh cilantro**
**3/4 cup diced red onions**
**2 garlic cloves, minced**
**1 tablespoon apple cider vinegar**
**2 tablespoons roasted peanut oil or toasted sesame oil**
**1 tablespoon brown sugar**
**Coarse salt and freshly ground black pepper to taste**

1. Roast the ears of corn over direct flame and cool. Cut the kernels from the cobs. There should be about 1 cup.

2. Toss all ingredients together in a glass or stainless steel bowl. Taste and adjust seasonings. Let stand at room temperature for 20 minutes. Serve.

# TOMATILLO-PAPAYA SALSA

This light fruity salsa is perfect for grilled fish or seafood. Try seared scallops for a real treat.

*Yield: 2-1/2 cups*

**4 tomatillos, peeled, rinsed, and cut into quarter-inch dice**

**1 ripe papaya, peeled, seeded, and cut into quarter-inch dice**

**2 serrano chiles, minced**

**1 small red bell pepper, cut into quarter-inch dice**

**1/2 cup diced red onion**

**1 tablespoon fresh lime juice**

**1 tablespoon fresh orange juice**

**2 tablespoons finely chopped fresh mint**

**1 tablespoon sugar, depending on the ripeness of the papaya**

**Coarse salt and freshly ground black pepper to taste**

1. Mix all ingredients in a stainless steel or glass bowl. Taste and adjust seasonings. It is best used within a few hours and doesn't hold well for more than a day.

*Tip: To use this as a more substantial side dish, add two to three cups of cooked basmati rice and season to taste with rice wine vinegar.*

# "HOLD ONTO YOUR HAT" HABANERO SALSA

Daniel Hoyer, restaurant consultant and seasoned chef at the Santa Fe School of Cooking, contributed this spirited salsa. He likes his salsas spicy, so beware! He recommends serving this with grilled shrimp, chicken, shredded beef, or pork tacos.

*Yield: 1-1/2 cups*

**3 fresh habanero chiles**

**2 garlic cloves, unpeeled**

**1/2 medium onion, peeled and cut into half-inch slices**

**4 ripe plum tomatoes**

**Juice of 1 small orange**

**Juice of 1 lime**

**1 teaspoon dried Mexican oregano**

**1/4 cup chopped fresh cilantro**

**1 tablespoon olive oil**

**Coarse salt to taste**

1. Roast the chiles, garlic, onion, and tomatoes over a direct flame until charred. Cool.

2. Peel the garlic and tomatoes. Remove stem and seeds and finely chop the chiles.

3. Place all the ingredients in the work bowl of a food processor and pulse, adding a few teaspoons of water as needed to yield a nicely spoonable consistency. Serve at room temperature or refrigerate until ready to use.

# KUMQUAT-HABANERO RELISH

This unique relish pairs well with oysters on the half shell, lobster, or monkfish. It would also add an unexpected sparkle to holiday dishes such as ham or goose.

*Yield: about 3 cups*

**12 ounces fresh kumquats, thinly sliced (about 3 cups)**

**1 habanero chile, stemmed and quartered**

**1 cup water**

**1 cup sugar**

**1/3 to 1/2 cup macadamia nuts, toasted and roughly chopped**

**2 tablespoons thinly sliced mint leaves**

**Pinch of salt**

**Squirt of fresh lime juice to balance the sweetness**

1. Bring water and sugar to a boil. Add the sliced kumquats and the habanero and simmer until the liquid is reduced to a syrupy consistency, about 10 minutes. If the relish seems too thick, stir in a tablespoon or two of water to thin. Cool.

2. Fold in the nuts and the mint. Season with salt and lime juice to taste. Serve at room temperature.

# NEW MEXICO RED CHILE SALSA

If you enjoy the smoky heat of chipotle chiles, this is the salsa for you. It's outstanding served on its own with tortilla chips, or with grilled pork or fajitas.

*Yield: 2-1/2 cups*

2 dried morita chiles or 2 tablespoons pureed,
   sieved chipotles in adobo sauce

8 dried New Mexico red chiles

4 medium-size ripe plum tomatoes

6 garlic cloves, unpeeled

1 medium white onion, peeled and cut into
   half-inch-thick slices

1 teaspoon crushed dried Mexican oregano

1/2 cup water

Salt to taste

Sugar to taste

Drizzle of extra virgin olive oil (optional)

1. Heat the broiler and set a heavy skillet over medium heat. Break the stems from the chiles and shake out the seeds. Place the chiles in the heated skillet, pressing them down with a kitchen towel until they have darkened in spots and you can smell their aroma. This process will take only moments. Place the toasted chiles in a bowl and pour very hot water over them. Weight them to submerge. Soak for 20 minutes, drain, and reserve the soaking water.

2. Spread the tomatoes on a foil-lined baking sheet and set on a rack positioned at the closest level to the broiler. Broil for 5 to 6 minutes, until softened and blackened. Using tongs, turn them over and roast for another 5 to 6 minutes, until softened and darkened on the other side. Cool, then peel the tomatoes, reserving any juices that accumulate and discarding the peelings.

3. Turn the oven down to 425 degrees. Separate the onion into rings. Spread the garlic and onion on a foil-lined baking sheet and roast until the garlic is soft and the onion is browned, about 15 minutes.

4. Chop the onion and garlic and set aside. Place the soaked chiles in a blender with a little of the soaking liquid; puree and reserve. Add the tomatoes and reserved juices to a food processor and pulse until coarsely pureed. Place the purees in a bowl and mix thoroughly. Add the oregano and water, if necessary, to give the salsa a pleasing consistency.

5. Taste and adjust seasonings with salt and sugar; drizzle with olive oil if desired.

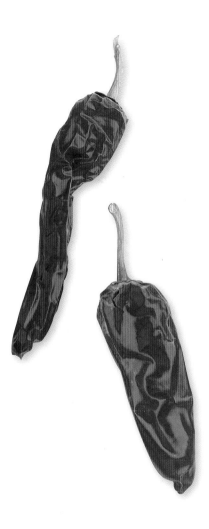

# TOMATILLO-AVOCADO SALSA

The light fresh flavor of uncooked tomatillos adds an interesting twist to the familiar guacamole. Serve with tortilla chips, tacos, or fajitas.

*Yield: 4 cups*

**1-1/2 pounds fresh tomatillos (about 12 to 14 medium),
    soaked in warm water and husked**

**1 medium white onion, peeled and cut into quarter-inch dice**

**2 garlic cloves, peeled and minced**

**2 or 3 fresh serrano chiles to taste, minced**

**1/2 cup coarsely chopped fresh cilantro**

**1 large ripe avocado**

**Juice from 2 or 3 limes, plus more to taste**

**Salt to taste**

**Sugar to taste**

**Extra virgin olive oil to taste**

1. Quarter the tomatillos and place in the work bowl of a food processor. Pulse to a coarse puree.

2. Place the tomatillos, onion, garlic, chiles, and cilantro in a bowl and stir to combine. Cut the avocado in half lengthwise, remove the pit, cube the flesh, and add to the tomatillos. Season with lime juice, salt, sugar, and drizzles of olive oil. Let stand 20 minutes. Taste and adjust seasonings.

# PICKLED RED ONIONS

Use these to brighten up a salad of watercress, pink grapefruit, and avocado, or use as a garnish for any Mexican dish. They work great to liven up a sandwich too.

*Yield: 2 cups*

1 cup red wine vinegar

1/2 six-ounce can frozen orange juice concentrate, thawed

1/4 cup sugar

1 teaspoon dried Mexican oregano

1 bay leaf

Salt to taste

Extra virgin olive oil to taste

4 medium-size or 2 large red onions,
    peeled and cut into slivers

1. Combine all ingredients except the onions in a large bowl and stir until the sugar is dissolved.

2. Bring 4 cups of water to a boil and add the onions. Let them sit for 3 minutes, then drain. Add the onions to the vinegar mixture and set aside at room temperature from 4 to 24 hours. Stir the mixture and refrigerate, covered. The onions will keep for several weeks or more. Drain to use.

# MANGO SALSA

This is a wonderful garnish for grilled tuna or salmon, or any fish taco. It can also be used as a base for an excellent fish salad by mixing about one pound of grilled tuna or salmon into the salsa.

*Yield: 3 cups*

2 large ripe mangoes

1 medium hothouse cucumber,* cut into quarter-inch dice

2 medium red bell peppers, roasted, peeled, seeded, and cut into quarter-inch dice

1 medium red onion, peeled and cut into quarter-inch dice

1/3 cup coarsely chopped fresh cilantro

2 to 3 serrano chiles, minced

Fresh lime juice to taste

Salt to taste

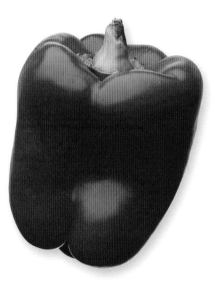

1. Peel the mangoes with a small sharp knife. Cut the flesh away from the large flat pit in two pieces, then cut it from the narrow edges of the pit. Cut these pieces into quarter-inch dice.

2. In a medium bowl, combine the diced mango, cucumber, red peppers, red onion, cilantro, chiles, lime juice, and salt. Toss gently but thoroughly.

3. Let the salsa stand at room temperature for 20 minutes to allow the flavors to meld. Serve at room temperature or slightly chilled.

*Regular cucumbers may be substituted, but peel and remove the seeds.*

# GRILLED PINEAPPLE SALSA

This is a popular recipe with everyone at the Santa Fe School of Cooking because it goes well with so many things. We suggest serving it with grilled salmon or tuna. It also complements turkey and is a lively accompaniment for ham. If you can't find a ripe pineapple, purchase a slightly green one and leave it at room temperature for several days to ripen.

*Yield: 2 to 2-1/2 cups*

1 medium-size ripe pineapple, peeled, cored, and cut lengthwise into half-inch-wide strips

Olive oil

Coarse salt and freshly ground black pepper to taste

1 large red bell pepper, cut into quarter-inch dice

1 medium red onion, peeled and cut into quarter-inch dice

2 to 3 serrano chiles, minced

1/3 cup coarsely chopped fresh cilantro (reserve some sprigs for garnish)

1 to 2 tablespoons freshly squeezed lime juice to taste

Pinch of sugar to taste, depending on the ripeness of the pineapple

1. Place the pineapple strips in a medium bowl and season with olive oil, salt, and pepper. Grill the strips until nicely marked but not too charred. Set aside to cool. Cut the strips into half-inch dice and return to the bowl.

2. Add the bell pepper, onion, chiles, cilantro, and lime juice; mix well. Taste and adjust seasonings. Set aside for 30 minutes. Serve.

*Tip: This is a basic recipe that works well with other tropical fruits. If ripe pineapple isn't available, substitute a ripe mango or papaya and avoid the mess of grilling.*

Note: Grilled Pineapple Salsa (lower left) and Mango Salsa (upper right).

# BING CHERRY-PISTACHIO SALSA

Zach Calkins, one of the more entertaining chefs at the Santa Fe School of Cooking, recommends serving this unusual fruit salsa with quail or game. It could also be incorporated into a stuffing for duck or goose, or used to garnish a cold soup of melon or cherries. It makes an excellent holiday accompaniment.

*Yield: 1-1/2 to 2 cups*

**8 ounces fresh bing cherries, stems and pits removed,**
   **or 10 ounces frozen bing cherries, thawed**
**1/2 cup shelled, toasted, roughly chopped pistachios**
**1/4 cup cilantro chiffonade**
**1 tablespoon juice from chipotle chiles in adobo sauce**
**Pinch of coarse salt to taste**
**Pinch of sugar to taste,**
   **or 1 to 2 teaspoons of Spicy Honey Whip to taste**
**1 to 2 teaspoons fresh lime juice to taste**

1. Roughly chop the cherries and stir in remaining ingredients. Season to taste with salt, sugar or honey, and lime juice. Serve.

# JICAMA-WATERMELON SALSA

A lovely perfumed combination of ripe watermelon, crisp jicama, spicy chile, fragrant herbs, and vanilla, this recipe was developed by Peter Zimmer, a past chef at the Santa Fe School of Cooking who opened the restaurant at the Inn of the Anasazi in 1990. It became an award-winning restaurant, which seems to be Peter's forte, as he has opened numerous award-winning restaurants around the country. Peter suggests serving this salsa with blackened salmon, barbecued pork tenderloin, chilled smoked jumbo prawns, or as a side salad.

*Yield: about 2 cups*

1 cup seeded and cubed ripe red or yellow watermelon

1/2 cup peeled and cubed jicama

1 small red onion, cut in thin slivers

1/4 cup New Mexico piñon nuts, toasted

1 ancho chile, stemmed, seeded, and cut with scissors into fine julienne

2 plum tomatoes, halved, insides scooped out, and shells cut lengthwise into thin strips

Zest of 1 orange

1 tablespoon mint chiffonade

2 tablespoons cilantro chiffonade

2 tablespoons rice wine vinegar

Seeds scraped from half a Mexican vanilla bean, pod reserved for another use

2 tablespoons Spicy Honey Whip or Red Chile Honey

1 tablespoon orange oil (optional)

Salt to taste

Sugar to taste

1. Combine all ingredients and let stand for 10 minutes. Taste and adjust seasonings. Serve well chilled.

# CHICOS, POSOLE, AND GRILLED ONION SALSA

Peter Zimmer, the creator of this truly southwestern salsa, has earned the title of the "Picasso of Food" at the school, as he creates magic with food not only in flavor but in appearance. He suggests serving this salsa with grilled meats or pork mole.

*Yield: 3-1/2 cups*

1/4 cup red posole

1/4 cup white posole

1/4 cup blue posole

1/4 cup chicos

1 small red onion, peeled and cut into half-inch slices

1 small Vidalia onion, peeled and cut into half-inch slices

2 large garlic cloves, unpeeled

1 small orange

1 lemon

1 lime

1 red pepper, roasted, peeled, seeded, and diced

1 yellow pepper, roasted, peeled, seeded, and diced

2 tablespoons green pumpkin seeds, toasted

2 small canned chipotle chiles in adobo sauce, finely chopped, or 1 tablespoon pureed chipotle chiles in adobo sauce

Pinch of ground cumin

1/2 teaspoon ground coriander

2 tablespoons mint chiffonade

1/3 cup cilantro chiffonade

2 tablespoons olive oil

Salt to taste

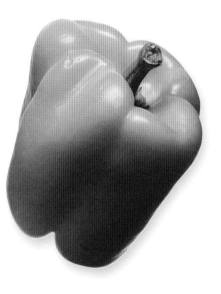

(continued on next page)

# CHICOS, POSOLE, AND GRILLED ONION SALSA

(continued from previous page )

1. Place the posole and chicos in a large saucepan and add 2 quarts of water. Bring to a boil and simmer for 2 to 3 hours, until the posole hulls have opened and the chicos are tender but chewy. Drain and rinse with cold water. Set aside.

2. Place the onions on a stove-top grill over a high flame and char lightly on both sides. Add the unpeeled garlic cloves to the flame and char on the outside. Set aside to cool. Peel the garlic cloves and mince. Coarsely chop the onions and mix with the garlic.

3. Juice and zest all the citrus fruits; fold into the peppers, seeds, chiles, cumin, coriander, the chiffonade of herbs, and olive oil. Then season to taste with salt.

4. Thoroughly combine the cooked posole, chicos, onions, and garlic with remaining ingredients in a medium-size bowl. Let stand for 30 minutes. Taste and adjust seasonings. Serve.

# ROASTED HABANERO PICKLED ONIONS

These onions are the perfect addition to all types of tacos and sandwiches. The addition of the fruity but **HOT** habanero chiles will give just the right amount of zing to the flavor.

*Yield: 2-1/2 cups*

1/3 cup good quality olive oil

2 large red onions, peeled and cut into thin slivers

2 fresh bay leaves

Leaves from 4 sprigs fresh marjoram

1/2 teaspoon dried Mexican oregano, lightly toasted

Coarsely ground black pepper to taste

Pinch of freshly ground allspice

1/4 cup balsamic or red wine vinegar

3 fresh habanero chiles, charred over a flame and chopped

Salt to taste

1. Heat olive oil in a large skillet over high heat. Saute the onions with the bay leaves for about 4 to 5 minutes, until lightly golden on the edges. Remove from the heat and stir in the marjoram, oregano, pepper, and allspice; combine thoroughly.

2. Stir in the vinegar and habaneros, and season to taste with salt. Set aside for 20 minutes. Serve at room temperature or chilled.

# LEMON CUCUMBER SALSA

Allen Smith, a former chef at the School, discovered lemon cucumbers while visiting Santa Fe's Farmers Market. At the time, he was living in New York City during what he describes as the "grilled meat and salsa rage." Allen created this recipe and thinks it serves as an easy way to "dress up" a simple piece of fish. It would also make a refreshing side salad.

*Yield: about 2 cups*

2 cups lemon cucumber,* unpeeled, cubed

Zest and juice of 1 lemon

2 green onions, trimmed and thinly sliced on the diagonal

2 teaspoons crushed red chile (chile caribe)

2 tablespoons chopped fresh herbs (a combination of
   chives, mint, tarragon, and/or cilantro is good)

Salt to taste

1. Combine all the ingredients and stir. Let stand for 20 minutes, taste,
   and adjust seasoning.

*Tip: Lemon cucumbers are named for their shape and color, which resemble lemons.
If you cannot find lemon cucumbers, peeled and seeded cucumbers may be substituted.*

# ROASTED PEPPER RAJAS

This salsa consists of roasted peppers and chiles cut into thin strips *(rajas)* and seasoned with sauteed garlic and fresh herbs. It is the perfect complement to grilled meats, fish, or pasta.

*Yield: about 2 cups*

1 red bell pepper, roasted, peeled, seeded, and cut into thin strips

1 yellow bell pepper, roasted, peeled, seeded, and cut into thin strips

1 orange bell pepper, roasted, peeled, seeded, and cut into thin strips

1 poblano chile, roasted, peeled, seeded, and cut into thin strips

2 large ripe plum tomatoes, halved, seeds scooped from the middle, and remaining shells cut lengthwise into thin strips

1 tablespoon chopped Italian parsley

1 tablespoon chopped fresh basil

2 tablespoons balsamic vinegar

Salt and freshly ground black pepper to taste

3 tablespoons extra virgin olive oil

2 cloves garlic, peeled and finely chopped

1. Place the pepper, chile, and tomato strips in a medium bowl along with the herbs, vinegar, salt, and pepper. Set aside.

2. Heat the olive oil in a small skillet over medium heat and saute the garlic until lightly golden and aromatic. Pour the oil and the garlic over the other ingredients and stir to combine well. Let stand for 10 minutes. Taste and adjust seasonings. Serve.

*Tip: During recipe-testing for the book, there were often leftover salsas and other odd ingredients. By adding raw shrimp to a skillet with this salsa, heating it until the shrimp were cooked, and adding a final dollop of heavy cream, a scrumptious lunch was prepared with the leftovers. Most salsas, unless very vinegary, serve as a good base for sauteed shrimp, scallops, cubed chicken, or a bit of meat.*

# ROASTED PEPPER RELISH
## WITH RAISINS AND PIÑON NUTS

This flavorful accompaniment enlivens pork tenderloin, lamb, or swordfish.

*Yield: about 2-1/2 cups*

1/3 cup golden raisins or currants

1/4 cup gold tequila

1 red bell pepper

1 yellow bell pepper

3 ripe plum tomatoes, cut into quarter-inch dice

1/3 cup thinly sliced scallions

2 tablespoons extra virgin olive oil

3 tablespoons diced red onion

1 cup diced zucchini or yellow squash

1 teaspoon minced garlic (optional)

1/3 cup New Mexico piñon nuts, lightly toasted

1/4 cup fresh herbs (basil, tarragon, cilantro, etc.), tightly packed and cut into chiffonade

2 to 3 tablespoons balsamic or red wine vinegar

Coarse salt and freshly ground black pepper to taste

1. Combine the raisins and tequila in a small saucepan and bring to a simmer over medium heat. Remove from the heat and set aside.

2. Char the bell peppers over a flame and place in a paper bag to cool for 10 minutes. Remove the skin, ribs, and seeds from the peppers and cut the flesh of the peeled peppers into thin strips. Cut the strips crosswise into quarter-inch dice and set aside in a small bowl. Add the tomatoes and scallions to the peppers.

3. In a small skillet over low heat, add the olive oil and saute the red onion about 3 minutes. Add to the peppers.

4. Drain the raisins, discarding any leftover tequila, and add to the relish with the remaining ingredients. Mix well and reserve at room temperature until ready to serve.

# GRAPEFRUIT-ORANGE SALSA

This colorful combination of citrus fruits makes a perfect condiment for fish tacos. The serranos add just the right chile kick. If serving a main dish intense with chile flavors, reduce the serranos so the salsa cools the palate.

*Yield: 6 servings*

**3 large oranges, peeled and sectioned**

**2 large Ruby Red grapefruits, peeled and sectioned**

**1/3 cup coarsely chopped fresh cilantro**

**1 to 2 serrano chiles, minced (optional)**

**1 red onion, trimmed and cut into slivers**

**Extra virgin olive oil to taste**

**Balsamic or red wine vinegar to taste**

**Salt to taste**

1. Combine all ingredients except the oil, vinegar, and salt; mix gently. Add the remaining ingredients no more than 5 minutes before serving (the acid will make the citrus sections fall apart).

*Serving suggestion: This salsa is a perfect side dish for duck and Monterey jack quesadillas.*

# ROASTED TOMATO SALSA

The flavor of this salsa is best in the summer, using red ripe tomatoes just picked from the vine. The tomatoes can easily be roasted on your outdoor grill in place of a stove-top grill. This salsa tastes terrific with just about anything; but for a real treat, try it with grilled lamb and fresh corn, or spoon over scrambled eggs for a whole new breakfast experience.

*Yield: about 3 cups*

2 pounds ripe plum tomatoes
3 garlic cloves, minced
1 large red onion, finely diced
2 to 3 serrano chiles, minced, or
    2 tablespoons pureed chipotle
    chiles in adobo sauce to taste
1/3 cup coarsely chopped fresh
    cilantro

1 teaspoon dried Mexican oregano,
    crushed
Splash of balsamic vinegar to taste
Coarse salt to taste
Pinch of sugar (optional)
Extra virgin olive oil to taste

1. Place a stove-top grill over high flame and char the plum tomatoes on all sides. Put them in a medium bowl and set aside to cool.

2. Peel and core the tomatoes. Place the tomatoes and their juices in the work bowl of a food processor and pulse to a coarse puree, keeping the tomatoes as chunky as possible. Pour the puree into a medium bowl. Add the garlic, onion, chile, cilantro, and oregano; season to taste with vinegar, salt, and sugar. Let stand for 20 minutes. Taste and adjust seasoning. Drizzle with a little olive oil, stir, and serve.

# FRESH TOMATO SALSA

Before the opening of the Santa Fe School of Cooking in December 1989, Bill Weiland, a local Santa Fe chef, was hired to help develop the first few recipes for the school. Susan Curtis, her husband David, and Bill congregated to test and taste a number of recipes. This "basic" fresh tomato salsa is one of the first recipes used at the school and is still very popular. Serve this salsa with chips or on tacos, enchiladas, or fajitas.

*Yield: about 2-1/2 cups*

**4 to 5 plum tomatoes, diced**

**1/2 cup finely chopped red onion**

**1 teaspoon dried Mexican oregano, crushed**

**2 serrano chiles, finely chopped**

**1 teaspoon minced garlic (optional)**

**3 tablespoons coarsely chopped fresh cilantro**

**2 to 3 tablespoons fresh lime juice or cider vinegar**

**1 tablespoon olive oil (optional)**

**Salt to taste**

**Pinch of sugar (optional)**

1. Put the tomatoes, onion, oregano, chiles, garlic, and cilantro in a bowl and mix well.

2. Add the lime juice or cider vinegar, olive oil, salt, and sugar to taste. Let the mixture sit for 20 minutes to meld the flavors.

# SALSA ROUGE

Chef Allen Smith was introduced to Salsa Rouge while a culinary student in France. As a guest at an Italian friend's house, he was served fettucini with olive oil and ground veal. At each place was a small ramekin of *salsa rouge*, similar to this delicious mixture. It makes a flavorful garnish for any meat or poultry, or can be used successfully as a quick sauce to spoon over pasta.

*Yield: 2 cups*

**1 red bell pepper, roasted, peeled, seeded, and diced**

**1 cup diced ripe tomato**

**1/2 cup chopped, oil-packed sundried tomatoes**

**1/3 cup chopped fresh basil**

**2 to 3 tablespoons red wine vinegar**

**2 to 3 tablespoons extra virgin olive oil**

**Salt to taste**

**Pinch of sugar to taste**

1. Combine all ingredients and let stand for 30 minutes. Taste and correct seasonings. Serve.

# TACO FILLINGS BOLD ON TASTE

It wouldn't be fair to provide you with recipes for such amazing salsas, and then leave you without any tacos. Hold on to your shoes because these taco fillings will knock your socks off! You will also create authentic homemade flour and corn tortillas. We've even added two simple salsas (you can never have too many salsas) at the end of the chapter plus side dishes like beans, spicy coleslaw and, of course, guacamole.

The mention of tacos may conjure up images of crispy corn tortillas filled with seasoned ground beef, lettuce, tomatoes, and cheese. Or you might think of a stand-up street stall in Mexico offering tacos of handmade soft tortillas topped with carne asada or carnitas, guacamole, and salsa. Both examples are genuine tacos, as is also a late-night snack of meats and sauces left over from a large meal and wrapped in tortillas. At the Santa Fe School of Cooking, we define a taco as any tasty filling served in or on flour or corn tortillas, crispy or soft.

While the use of chiles is important in many taco recipes, it doesn't mean you have to like your food spicy hot. Although chiles can provide that searing, sweat-producing heat that many of us enjoy, the flavor is more important than the fire. In Mexico, where the chile is revered, flavors are subtle rather than incendiary. Most often salsas and chiles are served on the side to allow guests to customize the piquancy. The following recipes allow for the enjoyment of chile flavor without forcing a tongue-numbing experience on unsuspecting guests. Taste the chile first, before you add it to a recipe. Climate and growing conditions can vary the intensity of chiles. In fact, two chiles from the same plant can have quite different levels of heat.

One thing is certain: tacos are fun! What better way to liven up a get-together than to serve an assortment of delicious taco fillings, homemade tortillas and a wide variety of salsas so everyone can create a customized meal? This chapter contains recipes from traditional to contemporary, chosen to help illustrate the limitless possibilities for preparing tacos. Enjoy our selections, and use your own creativity to develop variations and new favorites, for you, your family and friends to relish.

# ◈ INGREDIENTS FOR TACOS ◈

**Achiote Paste** — A seasoning condiment prepared from the ground seeds of the tropical annatto tree, mixed with garlic, spices, and vinegar. With an almost indescribable earthy flavor, achiote is used as a seasoning for seafood, meats, and poultry.

**Canela** — A soft variety of cinnamon originating in Ceylon (Sri Lanka). Lightly perfumed with a sweeter and less pungent flavor than the cinnamon commonly found in U.S. supermarkets, canela is used extensively in Mexico. Best if freshly ground canela is usually sold in stick form. Cinnamon may be used as a substitute for canela by halving the quantity called for in the recipe.

**Masa Harina** — The dry form of nixtamal, this masa is made from white corn that has been treated with mineral lime and then stone ground. Masa Harina is used to make fresh corn tortillas and tamales. It can be found in the Mexican food section in larger supermarkets.

(Also see Ingredients for Salsas on page 10 and Chiles on pages 13–14.)

# ◈ COOKING EQUIPMENT ◈

**Comal** — A heavy flat griddle, usually made of cast iron or ceramic material, that is used for cooking fresh corn and flour tortillas and for roasting chiles, vegetables, and spices.

**Santa Fe Grill** — The cooking school manufactures a grill that sits over the burner of gas and electric ranges. It can be used for roasting chiles, peppers, tomatoes, and garlic.

**Tortilla Press** — A handy piece of equipment, usually made from cast iron or aluminum, which is used to flatten masa when making fresh corn tortillas.

# PIPERADE BRUNCH TACOS

These tacos have their origin in the Basque egg dish called *Piperade*. Simple and easy to prepare, this filling adapts well to variations, so use your creativity. Serve them as a simple breakfast or as part of an elaborate feast.

*Yield: 16 to 18 tacos, 8 servings*

## Taco Filling

**1 medium onion, diced**

**3 tablespoons butter or olive oil**

**1 red pepper, diced, or a combination of red pepper and poblano or jalapeño chiles (may also be roasted and peeled before dicing)**

**1 clove garlic, peeled and minced**

**2 ripe tomatoes, cored and diced**

**1 teaspoon dried Mexican oregano, or 2 teaspoons chopped fresh herbs (like thyme or marjoram)**

**12 to 16 ounces chorizo, sliced or diced (a lightly cured, shaped sausage is best for this), or substitute smoked sausage or ham**

**8 large eggs, well beaten with salt and pepper**

**Grated cheese (optional)**

**Chile caribe (optional)**

## Tacos

**Flour or corn tortillas**

1. Saute onion in butter until golden in color. Add peppers and garlic; cook for 2 additional minutes.

2. Add tomato and oregano; cook 3 to 5 minutes more to evaporate most of the liquid.

3. Place chorizo in pan; saute for 2 to 3 minutes to heat and to release the fat.

4. Add beaten eggs and cook, stirring and scraping occasionally, to desired doneness.

5. Turn onto a warmed serving dish or platter and top with grated cheese and chile caribe if desired. Roll or fold in warm, homemade flour or corn tortillas.

*Serving suggestion: Great with sauteed potatoes, fresh fruit, and red and green salsas.*

# ADOBO PORK TACOS WITH GRILLED PINEAPPLE

Chef Daniel Hoyer fondly remembers eating these tacos on a hot October afternoon in Tequila, Mexico. He claims them in his "top ten" taco experiences. Maybe the tequila and the ice-cold cerveza helped too.

*Yield: enough for 24 tacos*

## Taco Filling

**4 pounds boneless, trimmed pork loin, cut in half-inch slices**
**1 medium white onion, chopped**
**2 ancho and 2 guajillo chiles, toasted, stemmed, and seeded**
**1 tablespoon puree of chipotle chiles in adobo**
**6 cloves garlic**
**1-1/2 ounces achiote paste**
**1/8 cup apple cider vinegar or rice wine vinegar**
**2 teaspoons honey**
**1/4 cup chopped fresh cilantro**

**1 tablespoon vegetable oil**
**4 cloves**
**1/4 cup water**
**1 teaspoon salt**
**1/2 teaspoon freshly ground black pepper**
**1 fresh ripe pineapple, peeled, cored, and cut lengthwise in half-inch-thick slices, then lightly brushed with vegetable oil**

## Tacos

**Corn tortillas**

1. Arrange slices of pork on a cutting board or smooth countertop between layers of plastic wrap. Using a meat-tenderizing mallet or a rolling pin, flatten the slices to form sheets about a quarter inch thick.

2. Place chiles, onion, garlic, achiote, vinegar, honey, cilantro, oil, water, cloves, salt, and pepper in a blender and puree smooth.

3. Spread mixture evenly over the sheets of pork and marinate in refrigerator for 1 to 3 hours. Remove from refrigerator 1/2 hour before cooking.

4. Preheat a charcoal or gas grill or oven broiler to produce a medium-high heat.

5. Place pineapple slices on grill alongside the marinated pork. Cook about 3 to 4 minutes on one side and turn over. Continue cooking until slightly charred and cooked through.

6. Remove from heat, cover and allow to rest for 5 to 10 minutes. Cut pork in quarter-inch strips. Garnish: pineapple may be sliced small as well or served in large slices.

7. Arrange on soft corn tortillas and top with garnishes.

*Serving suggestion: Serve with refried beans, Mexican rice, and an assortment of condiments such as roasted jalapeño chiles, Roasted Tomatillo Salsa, Mexican cheese, avocados, grilled onions, lime, and toasted oregano.*

# PORK CARNITAS TACOS

*Carnitas*, or "little meats," are very popular in Mexico and can be found in many parts of the United States as well. Many restaurants in Mexico feature carnitas on the weekends. Good carnitas are usually an indicator of an establishment's overall food quality. The traditional method of preparation can be an all-day process, but we have developed an approach that works well and is much easier. This recipe divulges a "secret" ingredient that many cooks use—Coca-Cola™—and we know of no substitute. If you don't have any or would rather not use it, simply replace the Coke™ with water; however, the carnitas will not brown as well.

*Yield: about 24 tacos*

## Taco Filling
**2 to 2-1/2 pounds pork stew meat or trimmed pork butt, cut into 1-inch cubes**
**4 ounces lard**
**1 teaspoon coarse salt**
**1 ancho chile, toasted, stems and seeds removed, and ground to powder (1-1/2 tablespoons)**
**1 guajillo or New Mexico red chile, toasted, stems and seeds removed, and ground to powder (1-1/2 tablespoons)**
**1 teaspoon ground, toasted cumin seed**
**6 whole allspice**
**3 whole cloves**
**6 cloves of garlic, peeled**
**2 bay leaves**
**1 cup Coca-Cola™ (not Diet Coke™)**
**2-1/2 cups meat broth or water**
**1 whole orange**

## Tacos
**Flour or corn tortillas**

1. Heat lard in a heavy saucepan until hot. (Don't use a pan that is too broad; a 10- or 12-inch bottom will keep the ingredients from spreading too far.)

2. Toss pork pieces with salt, ground chiles, and cumin seed. Cook in lard for 8 to 10 minutes, turning frequently to evenly brown.

3. Add allspice, cloves, garlic, and bay leaves, then the Coke™, broth or water, and whole orange.

4. Bring to a full boil, then reduce heat to just boiling. Cook, stirring occasionally, until most of the liquid has been absorbed and the lard is beginning to sizzle, about 1-1/4 hours. (The meat should be fork tender; if not, add more water and continue cooking).

5. Remove orange, turn heat up to medium high, and saute meat while stirring until pieces are well browned with caramelized edges. Remove from pan and drain well.

6. Serve with assorted condiments and fresh tortillas for build-your-own tacos. Carnitas are especially good with avocado or Guacamole.

# TACOS AL PASTOR

*Tacos al Pastor*, literally "shepherd's tacos," are filled with hearty stew-like meat. This is an adaptation from one of Santa Fe's favorite authentic Mexican restaurants, the Old Mexico Grill. Commercially in Mexico, the meat is cooked on a rotating spit and carved into thin slices to fill tacos, but we like this home-style approach created by this restaurant.

*Yield: 20 to 24 tacos, 8 to 10 servings*

## Taco Filling

4 ounces (about 8) dry ancho chiles, stemmed and seeded
2 cups water
3 to 4 roasted plum tomatoes, coarsely chopped,
    or 3/4 cup chopped canned tomatoes
2 tablespoons vegetable oil
3 pounds pork stew meat, trimmed and cubed pork butt,
    or cubed pork cushion meat
1/2 cup finely diced white onion
8 cloves of garlic, peeled and minced
1 tablespoon toasted dried Mexican oregano

1 teaspoon lightly toasted, ground cumin seed
1 teaspoon chopped fresh or dry thyme leaves (optional)
4 whole bay leaves
1 teaspoon freshly ground black pepper
1/8 cup apple cider vinegar or unseasoned
    rice wine vinegar
3/4 cup pineapple juice
2 teaspoons granulated sugar
1 teaspoon salt

## Tacos

Corn tortillas

1. Toast chiles on a skillet or comal or in a hot oven (425 degrees) until darkened slightly but not burned.

2. Bring water to a boil, add toasted chiles, stir well and remove from heat. Soak chiles for 15 to 20 minutes, drain and reserve water. Puree chiles in a blender with a little of the water and the tomatoes.

3. Heat oil in a 4- to 5-quart saucepan or in a pressure cooker. Brown meat a little at a time, remove, and reserve cooked pieces.

4. Add onions and then garlic and cook until onion is softened and begins to brown, about 2 minutes. Add oregano, cumin, thyme, bay leaves, and pepper along with chile-tomato puree and fry for one additional minute, stirring constantly.

5. Return browned pork to the pan and add vinegar, pineapple juice, sugar, salt, and 1 cup of reserved chile soaking water.

6. Bring to a boil, reduce heat, cover and cook for 35 minutes at 15 pounds in the pressure cooker. (Note: If using a regular pan, cook covered on low heat for about 1-1/2 hours until meat is tender. You may need to add water during the cooking process to prevent burning.)

7. Strain the sauce from the meat and cook longer, if needed, to thicken.

8. To serve, shred meat and place in soft corn tortillas. Garnish with chopped green onions and serve with Guacamole, some of the reserved sauce, Salsa Fresca, and lime wedges.

# COCHINITA PIBIL

*Pibil* is the Mayan word for the pit that is dug then lined with stones to roast a suckling pig. A fire is built and allowed to burn for several hours until it has been reduced to smoldering coals. Meanwhile, the *cochinita*, or little pig, has been seasoned and marinated with the exotic flavors of the brick-red achiote, the bright taste of citrus, and the floral heat of the habanero chile. Wrapped in banana leaves, the meat is placed in the pit, covered with the rocks and some palm leaves, and slow roasted overnight. This feast is then served family style with fresh handmade tortillas, salsas, condiments, and salads to make your own tacos.

Cochinita Pibil is a festive meal, excellent for parties and gatherings; the long, unattended cooking period allows time in the kitchen for the preparation of salsas, condiments, and side dishes. This recipe has been developed to provide the home cook with a close and quite good alternative to pit cooking. We have also had success with using the combination of a backyard smoker for 1-1/2 hours and the remainder of the time in the house oven. Although the banana leaves lend a distinct flavor to the meat as well as a dramatic presentation, a package of aluminum foil instead of leaves also produces an outstanding dish.

*Yield: about 3-1/2 pounds cooked meat, enough for 30 to 36 tacos*

## Taco Filling

1 medium, boneless pork butt (4 to 6 pounds), trimmed but with some fat remaining

3 ounces achiote paste

12 cloves peeled garlic

1 medium white onion, coarsely chopped (3/4 cup)

10 cracked allspice berries, or 2 teaspoons ground allspice

2 tablespoons toasted dried Mexican oregano

1 teaspoon toasted cumin seed

2 teaspoons cracked black pepper

6 bay leaves

2 tablespoons Worcestershire sauce

Juice of 2 limes

Juice of 1 orange

1/4 cup apple cider vinegar or rice wine vinegar

2 fresh habanero or Scotch bonnet chiles, stems and seeds removed, or 2 tablespoons bottled habanero chile sauce

2 tablespoons vegetable oil

1 teaspoon salt

1 package (1 pound) frozen banana leaves (available at specialty food stores and Latin American or Asian grocers). Thaw and rinse well in cool water. Tear 8 half-inch-wide strips off one leaf and tie two together to make four strips.

## Tacos

Corn tortillas

(continued on page 62)

# COCHINITA PIBIL

(continued from page 60)

1. Place pork in a freezer bag or other large plastic bag.

2. Mix all other ingredients except banana leaves in a blender or food processor. Pour in with pork, seal bag, and distribute well to coat meat. Marinate at least 2 hours or overnight in refrigerator.

3. Preheat oven to 325 degrees.

4. Line the bottom of a heavy roasting pan with 2 or 3 banana leaves. They should overlap the pan on all sides.

5. Remove pork roast from the bag and reserve marinade.

6. Place pork fat-side-up on banana leaves in the pan. Pour about 1/2 cup of marinade over top of meat.

7. Place 3 or 4 more leaves over pork and inside bottom leaves. Pull bottom leaves around meat; tie strips of banana leaves around this package from both directions to secure.

8. Bake at 325 degrees for 3-1/2 to 4 hours until meat is tender. Leaves may be almost black on the outside when finished.

9. Allow to cool for 20 minutes; then slit open banana leaves with a sharp knife or scissors (be careful of the steam) and remove pork.

*Serving suggestion: Fresh Corn Tortillas, habanero salsa, Pickled Red Onions, sliced radishes, chopped cilantro, citrus wedges, Guacamole, and jicama salad.*

# TACOS OF CALABACITAS

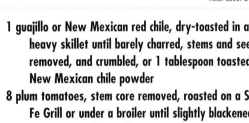

On the street in Mexico, these tacos are sometimes called *Entomates*, referring to the way the tortillas are dipped in a simmered tomato and chile sauce before they are cooked on the comal or griddle. Although they are tacos, they could also be described as enchiladas.

Calabacitas are prepared throughout the Southwest as well as in Mexico and are simply cut-up "little squash," generally summer varieties. Traditional preparations are varied, but this typical recipe features a combination of the squash and fire-roasted corn cooked with chiles and garlic.

*Yield: about 24 tacos*

## Sauce:

2 tablespoons vegetable oil

1/2 cup diced white onion

6 cloves garlic, peeled

2 teaspoons toasted dried Mexican oregano

1 ancho chile, dry-toasted in a heavy skillet until barely charred, stems and seeds removed, and crumbled, or 1 tablespoon toasted ancho chile powder

1 guajillo or New Mexican red chile, dry-toasted in a heavy skillet until barely charred, stems and seeds removed, and crumbled, or 1 tablespoon toasted New Mexican chile powder

8 plum tomatoes, stem core removed, roasted on a Santa Fe Grill or under a broiler until slightly blackened

1 teaspoon toasted ground cumin seed

1/2 to 3/4 cup water

Salt to taste

1. Preheat a heavy skillet or pan to medium heat and add oil. Add onion and garlic cloves; gently saute until onions are translucent and garlic is beginning to brown. Increase heat to high and add oregano, chiles, tomatoes, and cumin; fry for 1 minute more.

2. Add 1/2 cup of water and reduce heat to simmer.

3. Allow to cook for 15 minutes and place in a blender, adding more water if needed. Puree to a smooth consistency.

4. Return to pan and simmer for 30 minutes longer, adding more liquid as needed to prevent burning (finished sauce should be about as thick as good spaghetti sauce). Adjust for salt.

(continued on next page)

# TACOS OF CALABACITAS

(continued from previous page)

## Taco Filling

2 tablespoons butter or vegetable oil
1 teaspoon salt
2 zucchini squash, diced 3/8- to 1/2-inch square (about 1-1/2 cups diced)
2 yellow summer or crookneck squash, diced 3/8- to 1/2-inch square (about 1-1/2 cups diced)
5 cloves garlic, peeled and thinly sliced
1 teaspoon chopped fresh marjoram or toasted dried Mexican oregano
1/2 cup New Mexican green, Anaheim, or poblano chile, flame-roasted on a Santa Fe Grill, or under a broiler and peeled, or use chopped frozen New Mexican green chiles
1 cup roasted corn kernels or frozen corn kernels
1/2 cup water
Pepper to taste

## Tacos

24 to 28 fresh corn tortillas
8 ounces asadero or Monterey jack cheese, grated

1. Preheat a heavy saute pan or skillet to medium hot (325 to 345 degrees). Add oil or butter or a combination of the two.

2. Add squash and salt; cook, stirring often, for about 1 minute.

3. Add garlic and marjoram; cook for about 2 minutes more.

4. Add chiles, corn, water, and black pepper; continue cooking and stirring until most of the liquid has evaporated. Set aside until ready to assemble tacos.

When all ingredients are prepared, preheat a comal, griddle, or large skillet to medium hot (325 to 345 degrees). Brush the griddle with a light coating of vegetable oil, then dip a tortilla in the tomato sauce and place the tortilla on the comal. Place some calabacitas and 1/3 ounce of the cheese on the tortilla; fold in half. Cook on one side for about 1 minute, turn over, and continue cooking for 1 minute more. Repeat with remaining tacos. Serve immediately or reheat in a 350-degree oven. The leftover sauce may be poured over the tacos for garnish.

*Serving suggestions: This is excellent as a side dish with roasted chicken or as a buffet course.*

# HOT AND SMOKY SHRIMP TACOS

The flavor and the spiciness of chipotle chiles, which are smoked red jalapeños, make a perfect foil for the garlicky shrimp. This dish was meant to be hot, but you can vary the intensity of heat by reducing the quantity of chile. If you like, the shrimp may also be prepared using an outdoor grill; make the sauce without the shrimp, then brush some on the shrimp before grilling. Toss shrimp with the remaining sauce after they are cooked.

*Yield: 20 to 25 tacos, 8 to 10 servings*

## Taco Filling
3 tablespoons olive oil
1 tablespoon butter
8 cloves garlic, sliced
1-1/2 pounds medium shrimp (26 to 30 per pound),
    peeled and deveined
1-1/2 teaspoons coarse salt
1/8 to 1/4 cup (some like it hot!) pureed chipotle
    chiles in adobo

1/2 cup roasted tomato puree or canned tomato sauce
2 tablespoons cold water
Juice of 1/2 orange
Juice of 1 lime
1/2 cup chopped cilantro (about 1/2 large bunch)
## Tacos
Fresh corn tortillas

---

1. Preheat a heavy skillet or saute pan to medium hot (325 degrees); add olive oil and butter and continue heating until oil begins to smoke (400 degrees). Immediately add garlic, shrimp, and salt, stirring or tossing vigorously. Oil tends to splatter at this temperture, so be careful.

2. When shrimp begin to turn opaque, stir in the chipotle chile puree and saute about 15 seconds to completely coat shrimp.

3. Add tomato puree, water, and orange and lime juices.

4. Reduce heat slightly and bring to a boil for 1 minute. Remove from heat and stir in cilantro.

5. Serve in fresh soft corn tortillas, 2 or 3 shrimp per taco.

*Serving suggestion: Garnish tacos with shredded romaine lettuce, Salsa Verde, sliced avocados, radishes, lime wedges, and a dollop of sour cream. Serve with white rice and black beans.*

# CHARGRILLED FISH TACOS WITH CARIBBEAN SEASONINGS

On the island of Cozumel and throughout the Yucatan, achiote is a favorite seasoning for fresh fish. We have combined it with other exciting tropical flavors for a seasoning rub for fish tacos. This seasoning also works great for shrimp, chicken, and turkey. The chargrill adds a hint of smoke, but this dish can be prepared in the oven or saute pan also.

*Yield: 18 tacos, 6 to 8 servings*

**Taco Filling**
3 to 3-1/2 pounds red snapper filets (or other firm-fleshed fish: red rockfish, tuna, mahi-mahi, sea bass), preferably fresh
2 ounces achiote paste
4 cloves garlic
Juice and zest of 1 lime
All of the juice and half of the zest of 1 orange
6 allspice berries, or 1-1/2 teaspoons ground allspice
1/2 teaspoon freshly ground black pepper

1 teaspoon coarse salt
4 tablespoons fresh cilantro leaves
1 fresh habanero chile, stemmed and seeded, or 1 tablespoon bottled habanero sauce
1 tablespoon apple cider vinegar or rice wine vinegar
1 tablespoon honey
2 tablespoons vegetable oil
1 tablespoon water

**Tacos**
Corn or flour tortillas

1. Place all filling ingredients except fish in a blender and puree smooth.

2. Evenly coat the fish filets with achiote mixture; cover and allow to marinate at room temperature for 20 to 30 minutes.

3. Cook fish on a charcoal or gas grill or in the oven broiler for approximately 3 minutes per side, depending on thickness of filets. (We think fish tastes best when cooked medium rare to medium, especially when it is very fresh.)

4. Allow to cool for a few minutes and slice for tacos.

5. Serve in soft corn or flour tortillas.

*Serving suggestions: Garnish with a fresh fruit or tomato-habanero salsa or Pickled Red Onions and lime wedges.*

# BAJA-STYLE FISH TACOS WITH CHIPOTLE MAYONNAISE

Rubio's Baja Grill in San Diego started the fish taco craze north of the border in 1983 when Ralph Rubio transplanted his favorite recipe from a small taco vendor on the Baja coast to his southern California restaurant. We are sharing our version of this beachside treat.

*Yield: 16 generous tacos*

## Taco Filling

**1-1/2 pounds cod filets (or other firm white fish), cut in 2-1/2- by 1/2-inch pieces**
**8 ounces full-flavored pale ale or Mexican lager**
**3 whole eggs, well beaten**
**2 teaspoons Coleman's dry mustard**
**1 tablespoon New Mexican or other red chile powder**
**1 tablespoon salt**
**2 teaspoons sugar**
**1-1/2 cups all-purpose flour + 1 cup for dredging**
**Oil for frying (preferably canola or peanut oil)**

## Tacos

**Flour tortillas**

1. Mix half of the beer with all other ingredients except fish and blend well with a whisk.

2. When all lumps have been smoothed, continue adding beer until a slightly thinner-than-pancake-batter consistency is attained. Keep chilled at all times.

3. Dredge fish filets in flour and dip in batter, being careful to completely coat. Allow excess to drip off.

4. Fry in 350-degree oil for 2-1/2 to 4 minutes, until golden brown and cooked through.

5. Drain well and allow to cool slightly.

6. When ready to serve, heat flour tortillas and place in a towel or cloth to keep warm. Re-fry the fish for about 1 more minute to make it crispy.

7. Spread tortillas with a tablespoon of Chipotle Mayonnaise (see below); add Spicy Coleslaw or shredded lettuce, several pieces of fish, and guacamole or salsa if desired.

## Chipotle Mayonnaise

**1 cup mayonnaise**
**Juice of 1 lime**
**1 tablespoon chopped cilantro**
**1/8 teaspoon salt**
**1 tablespoon pureed chipotle chiles in adobo**

1. Mix all ingredients well and refrigerate.

# POLLO IN SALSA VERDE

Salsa Verde is a classic Mexican sauce that complements leftover cooked chicken and turkey, and also works well with sauteed shrimp or scallops. The lemony tartness of the tomatillos is balanced by the natural sweetness of the cooked garlic and onions with a little help from the sugar.

*Yield: 20 to 24 tacos, 8 to 10 servings*

### Taco Filling
3/4 pound fresh tomatillos (about 8), husked and rinsed
    under hot tap water for 30 seconds
3 tablespoons vegetable oil
1/2 white onion, chopped
1 or 2 fresh jalapeño chiles, stems removed and sliced
4 cloves garlic, peeled
1/2 teaspoon salt
1 teaspoon granulated sugar
2 teaspoons chopped fresh epazote or marjoram,
    or 1 teaspoon toasted dried Mexican oregano

1 teaspoon apple cider vinegar or rice wine vinegar
1/2 cup water
2 or 3 chiles de arbol or other small dry red chiles,
    toasted, stemmed, and seeds removed
2 pounds (about 8 to 10 pieces) boneless chicken thighs,
    cut into 1-inch-square pieces
1 teaspoon chile powder (optional)
Salt and pepper to taste

### Tacos
6 ounces asadero or Monterey jack cheese, grated
Corn tortillas

1. Roast the tomatillos on a Santa Fe Grill, in a very hot oven, or under a broiler until about half of the surfaces are well charred.

2. In a preheated skillet or heavy saucepan, add 1 tablespoon of oil, onions, jalapeño slices, and garlic; saute until onions are slightly browned and beginning to soften.

3. Place in a blender with roasted tomatillos, salt, sugar, herbs, vinegar, water, and dry chiles. Puree smooth.

4. In the same skillet or pan, add remaining oil and heat until just beginning to smoke (very hot). Season chicken pieces with chile powder, salt, and pepper; cook until browned on all sides.

5. Pour in sauce puree, stir well, and reduce heat to simmer. Cook, stirring occasionally, for about 10 to 12 minutes. Remove from heat. Sauce should be fairly thick.

6. Place soft corn tortillas on a baking sheet, top with chicken mixture and about a tablespoon of grated cheese. Place under a broiler or in a very hot oven (475-degree) until cheese is bubbly and starting to brown.

*Serving suggestion: Try this with corn-and-black-bean salsa and oven-roasted garlic potato wedges for a delicious light supper.*

# SANTA FE WRAPS

Most tacos and burritos could also be called wraps, but what we are referring to here is a contemporary hybrid of a sandwich and a burrito. Wraps are wonderfully versatile. They can be made in advance, and they travel well for picnics or boxed lunches. When cut into smaller pieces, they make tasty appetizers. The following are two examples of wraps similar to ones that we developed for the newly launched "Santa fe" restaurant chain in London, England.

# GRILLED VEGETABLE WRAP

*Yield: 6 servings of 2 pieces each, or 4 dozen small slices for appetizers*

## Wrap Filling
1/8 cup olive or vegetable oil
1 tablespoon chile caribe or dry crushed red peppers, toasted
6 cloves garlic, peeled and minced
2 tablespoons chopped mixed fresh herbs (cilantro, marjoram, chives, thyme, oregano, etc.), or 1-1/2 tablespoons toasted dried Mexican oregano
2 medium zucchini squash, ends trimmed and cut lengthwise into quarter-inch-thick slices
2 medium yellow summer or crookneck squash, ends trimmed and cut lengthwise into quarter-inch-thick slices

1 Japanese eggplant, peeled and cut lengthwise into quarter-inch-thick slices
2 sweet bell peppers (red or yellow), ends cut, stemmed and seeded, membranes removed, cut into long quarters
2 poblano, New Mexican green, or Anaheim chiles, ends cut, stemmed and seeded, membranes removed, cut into long quarters
2 teaspoons coarse salt
Freshly ground black pepper
1/2 cup Chipotle Crema + extra for dipping

## Tacos
6 nine- to ten-inch-diameter or 8 eight-inch-diameter flour tortillas, flavored or plain

1. Mix oil, chile caribe, garlic, and herbs; let sit for at least 15 minutes to allow flavor to develop.

2. Salt and pepper sliced vegetables and place in a plastic bag or large bowl. Add oil mixture and coat vegetables evenly. Marinate for 30 minutes or overnight.

3. Cook over a charcoal or gas grill or in the oven broiler until slightly browned, cooked through but not too soft.

4. Heat tortillas one by one over a gas flame or on a comal or skillet. Spread each with 1 tablespoon of Chipotle Crema, arrange a mixture of cooked vegetables in the center, and wrap tightly to form a cylinder.

5. With a sharp knife, slice each filled tortilla in half diagonally, or slice into 8 to 10 pieces for hors d'oeuvres.

6. Serve with additional Chipotle Crema for dipping.

*Note: It takes 24 to 30, 2 x 6 x 1/4-inch slices of grilled vegetables to make 6 wraps.*

# CHICKEN AL CARBON AND AVOCADO WRAP

*Yield: 6 servings of 2 pieces each, or 4 dozen small slices for appetizers*

## Wrap Filling

**4 boneless, skinless chicken breasts (7 to 8 ounces in size)**
**Juice of 1 lime**
**1 tablespoon vegetable oil**
**Salt and pepper to taste**
**1 tablespoon chipotle powder or other red chile powder**
**1/2 cup Chipotle Crema + extra for dipping**
**1-1/2 cups shredded romaine lettuce**
**1 cup Salsa Fresca (see p. 90) or other favorite salsa**
**2 to 3 medium-size ripe avocados, peeled, pitted, and sliced**

## Tacos

**6 nine- to ten-inch-diameter or 8 eight-inch-diameter flour tortillas, flavored or plain**

1. Sprinkle chicken breasts with lime juice, then coat with oil. Season with salt, pepper, and chile powder. Allow to sit 10 to 15 minutes.

2. Cook on a charcoal or gas grill or in the oven broiler until just cooked through, about 3 to 4 minutes per side.

3. Allow to rest for 10 minutes, then slice lengthwise in half-inch-wide strips.

4. Heat tortillas one by one over a gas flame or on a comal or skillet. Spread each with 1 tablespoon of Chipotle Crema; in the center, place some lettuce, salsa, chicken slices, and avocado; wrap tightly to form a cylinder.

5. With a sharp knife, slice each filled tortilla in half diagonally, or slice into 8 to 10 pieces for hors d'oeuvres.

6. Serve with additional Chipotle Crema for dipping.

## Chipotle Crema

**1-1/2 cups sour cream**
**3 tablespoons milk or cream**
**Juice of 1 lime**
**1/4 teaspoon salt**
**2 tablespoons chopped fresh cilantro**
**1 tablespoon or more pureed chipotle chiles in adobo to taste**

1. Mix all ingredients together and chill. The crema tends to thicken over time. Thin with milk or cream as desired.

*Note: We prefer the smoky-hot richness of chipotle chile here, but it can be made with other hot sauces as well.*

# CREAMY CHICKEN AND ALMOND TACOS

Almonds and olives are two old-world ingredients that have been embraced by cooks in Mexico. The richness of the cream balances nicely with the Mediterranean-style filling.

*Yield: 18 to 20 tacos*

## Taco Filling
**1 medium white onion, diced**
**4 tablespoons olive oil**
**1 cup diced fresh tomato or canned diced tomato**
**2 cloves garlic, minced**
**3 cups cooked and diced chicken breast**
    **(3 to 4 medium-size breasts)**
**1/4 cup sliced blanched almonds**
**1 tablespoon capers**
**2 tablespoons coarsely chopped raisins**

1. Saute onion in olive oil until golden brown. Add tomatoes and cook for 3 to 4 minutes more.

2. Mix in additional ingredients, heat through, and set aside while preparing sauce.

## Tacos
**18 to 20 corn tortillas**

1. Heat corn tortillas one at a time, place about 2 tablespoons of the warm chicken filling in each one, and roll into a cylinder.

2. Arrange tacos on a serving platter and cover with cream sauce. Garnish with chopped fresh cilantro or flat-leafed parsley.

## Cream Sauce
**1 small white onion, diced**
**4 tablespoons butter**
**1 poblano chile, roasted, peeled, and diced**
**1 green or red bell pepper, roasted, peeled, and diced**
**1 or 2 jalapeño chiles, stemmed, seeded, and minced**
**2 cups heavy or whipping cream**
**1 cup grated Monterey jack cheese**
**1/2 cup sliced pimento-stuffed green olives**
**Salt to taste**

1. Saute onion in butter until softened. Add chiles and pepper dices; cook for an additional 3 to 4 minutes.

2. Pour in cream; bring to a boil, then reduce heat and simmer until cream is thick enough to coat the back of a spoon.

3. Stir in grated cheese and heat until completely melted. Remove from heat and mix in sliced olives. Adjust for salt.

# FIRE-ROASTED CORN AND POBLANO CHILE TACOS

This dish takes its inspiration from the ubiquitous Mexican street-vendor treat *Esquites*. Made from fresh ears of sweet white corn roasted over a charcoal fire, the esquites are cut off the cob and served in a cup with chiles, lime, and crumbled cheese. When used for a taco filling, the flavors of the fresh corn and the corn tortilla contrast as well as complement each other.

*Yield: 24 tacos, 8 servings*

## Taco Filling

6 ears fresh white or yellow corn,
  or 3-1/2 cups of frozen corn kernels may be
  substituted if fresh corn is not available
1 tablespoon butter
1/2 medium white onion, finely diced
3 cloves garlic, peeled and sliced
3 medium to large poblano chiles, roasted,
  peeled, stemmed, seeded, and diced
Dash of salt

1 teaspoon toasted dried Mexican oregano,
  or 1 teaspoon chopped fresh marjoram
3/4 cup half-and-half, or 2/3 cup heavy cream
Juice of 1 lime
6 ounces grated Monterey jack cheese
3 ounces Mexican cotija, Romano, or
  Parmesan cheese, grated

## Tacos

2 tablespoons vegetable oil
Soft corn tortillas

1. Roast corn in the husk until just tender (about 10 minutes over charcoal or 18 minutes in a 425-degree oven), cool, husk, and strip.

2. Heat butter in a heavy saute or saucepan over medium-high heat. Cook onion for 1 to 2 minutes, until slightly browned on the edges. Add garlic and saute for 1 minute more.

3. Add poblano chiles, corn, salt, and oregano. Stir to combine and add half-and-half. Bring to a boil and reduce heat to simmer. Reduce liquid by half (by a third if using cream), stirring often.

4. Add lime juice and cheeses and heat through until bubbly; mixture will be fairly thick.

5. Preheat griddle, comal, or heavy skillet to medium-high heat, then brush with a light coating of oil.

6. Place tortillas a few at a time on hot surface and spoon 1-1/2 tablespoons of the mixture on top of each. When tortillas are softened, fold over to make tacos. Cook until golden brown on both sides; place in a cloth-lined basket or serving dish and cover. Repeat with remaining tacos.

*Note: The filling may be made in advance and refrigerated.*

*Suggested accompaniments: Roasted Tomato Salsa, Frijoles Charros, and a crispy salad.*

# CARNE ASADA

Carne Asada is known throughout Mexico and has become somewhat of a national dish. The most famous recipe originated in the Gulf Coast port of Tampico and was made popular by several Mexico City high-style eateries in the past century. Beef tenderloin is used in the more expensive restaurants but other cuts are commonly served at taquerias and street taco stands. Like many other traditional taco meals, the condiments and accompaniments are what make this special.

Bert's Taqueria in Santa Fe presents their tacos in an authentic Mexico City style, with various condiments and a changing selection of salsas. The owner, Fernando Olea Caballero, graciously loaned us the comal from his restaurant that we used in the photograph.

*Yield: 6 to 8 servings*

## Taco Filling
2-1/2 pounds sirloin steak, chuck steak, or beef tenderloin
Juice of 3 limes
3 tablespoons olive or vegetable oil
1 tablespoon chipotle chile powder
1 to 2 fresh jalapeño or serrano chiles, thinly sliced
3 cloves garlic, minced

1 scallion, chopped
Freshly ground black pepper
2 teaspoons salt
8 fresh green onions (scallions), washed, trimmed, and coated with a small amount of vegetable oil

## Tacos
Flour or corn tortillas

1. Trim meat of excess fat and slice or "butterfly" the meat into a sheet about 3/8-inch thick (your butcher can do this for you).

2. Place the meat between 2 sheets of plastic wrap and carefully pound it with a meat-tenderizer mallet or rolling pin to a quarter-inch thickness.

3. Coat with lime juice and brush lightly with oil. Sprinkle chile powder, jalapeño chiles, garlic, scallions, and black pepper evenly on both sides of the meat.

4. Allow to marinate for 20 to 30 minutes.

5. Salt and cook on chargrill or griddle alongside the whole green onions until beef is just cooked through and onions are beginning to brown.

6. Allow meat to rest for 5 minutes.

7. Slice the beef in long thin slices approximately a quarter-inch thick.

8. Arrange on plate, top with grilled green onions, and garnish with lime wedges.

9. Serve with warm tortillas, black beans, and/or calabacitas.

*Suggested condiments: Salsa Fresca or Salsa Verde, toasted dried Mexican oregano, chopped fresh cilantro, Guacamole, sliced cucumbers and radishes, pickled or roasted jalapeño chiles, lettuce, and such crumbly cheeses as queso fresco or cotija.*

# STEAK AND MUSHROOM TACOS WITH GREEN CHILES

The Pink Adobe is one of Santa Fe's oldest and most popular restaurants. Chef and owner Rosalea Murphy has developed several innovative recipes that have become favorites with both locals and visitors. Her Steak Dunigan reflects the cultural fusion that has been an integral part of the city's colorful past and continues even today. Pairing the earthy flavors of mushrooms with the enticing aroma and spiciness of fire-roasted green chiles to complement the culinary icon of the West—the chargrilled steak—is nothing short of brilliant. These flavors work so well together that we have borrowed from Rosalea's original idea to create this taco recipe.

*Yield: about 24 tacos*

## Taco Filling
**2 pounds sirloin or other favorite cut of steak**
**5 tablespoons olive oil**
**4 cloves garlic, minced**
**2 tablespoons chopped fresh marjoram, thyme, or toasted dried Mexican oregano**
**Juice of 1 lime**
**Salt and freshly ground black pepper to taste**

**1-3/4 cups (8 ounces) sliced mushrooms (substitute or mix other varieties such as shiitake, portabello, crimini, etc.)**
**1 medium onion, thinly sliced**
**1 cup green chiles, diced, roasted, and peeled (depending on the season, use New Mexican, Anaheim, or poblano chiles; frozen green chiles also work well)**

## Tacos
**Corn or flour tortillas**

1. Marinate steak at room temperature for 30 minutes in 3 tablespoons of olive oil mixed with garlic and herbs.

2. Remove from marinade and liberally salt and pepper the steak. Cook on a chargrill or in a broiler until rare to medium rare. Allow steak to rest for 15 minutes. Cut into half-inch-wide strips and slice thinly across the strips to produce bite-size slices.

3. Place 2 tablespoons oil in a preheated skillet on medium high. When oil is very hot, add mushrooms and saute for 1 minute, stirring several times. Add onions and continue for about 2 to 3 minutes more, until slightly browned. Cook the steak slices with mushrooms and onions for 2 to 3 minutes more, then mix in green chiles. When chiles are heated through, remove from heat and serve.

*Serving suggestion: Accompany with Fresh Corn or Flour Tortillas, assorted condiments, cheeses, salsa, salad, and refried beans.*

# TACOS DE LENGUA

Noe Cano is the sous chef at the cooking school. Originally from Vera Cruz on the Gulf Coast of Mexico, Noe is appreciated by all of the instructors for his cooking skills and attention to detail. He contributed this easy-to-prepare and very tasty recipe, and even managed to convert some skeptical members of our taste panels.

In many countries, virtually every part of the animal is consumed. People are quite aware of what they are eating; in fact, many prefer these variety meats to the everyday cuts that the U.S. consumer tends to favor. Restaurants in Mexico commonly offer a variety of taco fillings that may include liver, kidneys, sweetbreads, cabeza (steer or hog's head), tripe, pig's feet, and an assortment of sausages.

*Yield: 24 to 30 tacos*

**Taco Filling**
2-1/2 to 4 pounds of calf or beef tongue
12-ounce bottle of Mexican lager
Enough water to cover the meat
2 bay leaves
1 white onion, coarsely chopped, about 3/4 cup
    (reserve half for final cooking step)
3 cloves peeled garlic

1 teaspoon whole black peppercorns
4 whole cloves
1 teaspoon salt
2 dry hot chiles (chile de arbol, pequin, or Japonese)
3 tablespoons vegetable oil or lard

**Tacos**
Corn tortillas

1. Place tongue in a large braising pan or pot; add beer and enough water to just cover. Bring to a boil; cook for 5 minutes, remove from heat, and skim any foam or solids that are floating on the surface.

2. Add rest of the ingredients except for reserved onion; return to a boil, then reduce heat to simmer, adding water as needed. Allow 45 minutes of cooking time per pound of meat. Completely cool tongue in the cooking liquid.

3. With a sharp knife, make an incision the length of the top side. Peel away the outer layer with your fingers or carefully with the knife. Slice 1/4- to 3/8-inch thick, then cut across and diagonally to produce square cubes.

4. Heat lard on high in a preheated skillet or saute pan. Stir-fry cubed meat with the remaining onions, a dash of salt, and freshly ground pepper. When meat is well browned serve with freshly made Corn Tortillas with Salsa Verde and cotija or other favorite crumbly cheese.

# ROASTED WILD MUSHROOM TACOS WITH QUESO FRESCO

In the markets of Oaxaca you can see basketsful of multicolored fresh mushrooms for sale—some familiar, some not. Queso fresco is a slightly aged, crumbly, mild, farmer-style Mexican cheese. Feta or mild fresh goat cheese may be used for a stronger flavor. This recipe has been adapted from a favorite of Zach Calkins, a former chef/instructor at the cooking school.

*Yield: 24 soft tacos*

**Taco Filling**
3 cloves garlic, peeled
1/4 cup olive oil
4 cups thickly sliced (about 3/8-inch thick),
    stemmed wild mushrooms (any combination
    of shiitake, chanterelle, oyster, portobello, or
    Italian brown mushrooms)

2 teaspoons fresh or dry epazote,
    or substitute toasted dried Mexican oregano
1/2 teaspoon salt
1/2 teaspoon freshly ground black pepper
3 blackened serrano chiles, stems removed and minced
8 ounces queso fresco or other mild crumbly cheese
**Tacos**
Soft corn tortillas

1. Puree garlic with olive oil in a blender or food processor; allow to sit for 10 minutes to infuse the flavor. Strain and discard garlic.

2. Brush mushrooms clean, then toss with infused olive oil, epazote, salt, and pepper. Spread on a cookie sheet or a cast-iron skillet; place in a preheated 425-degree oven and roast until browned and caramelized along the edges, about 8 to 10 minutes. Remove from oven.

3. Immediately toss with serrano chiles and cheese.

4. Place on heated corn tortillas, fold, and serve.

*Note: Up to half of the wild mushrooms may be replaced with domestic white mushrooms to reduce the cost.*

*Serving suggestions: Saffron rice, Caesar salad, and your favorite salsa make these tacos perfect for a light supper, or serve them as an accompaniment to roasted meats.*

# POTATO, POBLANO CHILE, AND SPINACH TACOS WITH CREAM

These tasty tacos are enjoyed in classes at the cooking school. They are also featured at one of Daniel's favorite taco restaurants in Oaxaca. The filling can be made in advance and kept refrigerated for several days. Beware—even though they are very rich, many people won't be satisfied with only two.

*Yield: about 5 cups of filling, enough for 20 to 24 tacos*

## Taco Filling
1 pound waxy boiling potatoes (about 4 to 5 red or white rose potatoes)
1 large white onion, diced
2 tablespoons vegetable oil
4 cloves garlic, peeled and sliced
2 bunches fresh spinach, washed, stems trimmed, and coarsely chopped
1 teaspoon toasted dried Mexican oregano, or 2 teaspoons chopped fresh oregano or marjoram

4 fresh poblano chiles, roasted, seeded, peeled, and cut into quarter-inch strips about 2 inches long
1 cup heavy cream, good quality sour cream, or Mexican cream
1 cup grated cheese (Monterey jack, cotija, Parmesan, fontina, or a mix)
Salt to taste

## Tacos
Corn Tortillas

1. Peel potatoes and dice into 3/8-inch cubes. Cook in boiling salted water until potatoes are soft but not falling apart, about 10 to 12 minutes.

2. Heat oil in a medium-hot skillet; lightly brown onions, then add garlic and boiled potatoes and cook for 2 more minutes. Begin adding spinach a handful at a time, stirring with tongs to wilt it. When all the greens are wilted, add herbs, poblano chiles, and cream.

3. Cook on low boil, stirring occasionally, until liquid is reduced by a third; stir in cheese and continue cooking until smooth and thick. Adjust salt if needed.

4. Place in a serving dish along with a basket of warm corn tortillas so that guests may assemble their own tacos. Tomato salsas are excellent with these rich and creamy tacos.

# FRESH CORN TORTILLAS

Yield: 22 to 24 three-and-a-half-inch tortillas

**2 cups dry masa harina (available from the cooking
    school and at many supermarkets)**
**1/2 teaspoon salt**
**1-1/3 cups (approximately) warm water
    (95 to 115 degrees)**

1. Place dry ingredients in a mixing bowl and slowly add water while stirring with a fork until dough forms a ball. Knead dough several times by hand until smooth, then form into a 2-inch-thick log. Wrap in plastic and let stand for about 30 minutes.

2. Preheat a comal, heavy skillet, or griddle to medium high (350 degrees).

3. Slice masa dough into just under 1/2-inch-thick rounds and cover to prevent drying.

4. Place a round between two sheets of plastic (a freezer bag split into 2 sheets works well) and flatten in a tortilla press to about 1/16 inch thick.

5. Peel off top sheet of plastic and gently drop tortilla from the other sheet by inverting it over the comal or griddle. Cook for about 1 minute and turn over. Cook for 30 seconds more, pushing down with a spatula several times. Cooked tortillas should have light brown speckles.

6. Keep cooked tortillas in a kitchen towel or cloth napkin to keep warm while cooking others and for serving. Serve immediately.

*Note: This recipe may be prepared using a food processor. Place the dry ingredients in a bowl fitted with a steel blade. While processor is running slowly, pour the warm water through the feed and process until a smooth dough ball is formed. Proceed as above.*

# FRESH FLOUR TORTILLAS

Yield: 8 to 10 five-inch tortillas

**2 cups all-purpose flour**
**1/2 teaspoon salt**
**1-1/2 teaspoons baking powder**
**3 tablespoons vegetable shortening**
**3/4 cup hot water (145 degrees or more)**

1. Combine dry ingredients in a bowl and mix well.

2. Cut in the shortening until mix is the consistency of coarse cornmeal.

3. Add water and mix to form a soft but not too sticky dough.

4. Knead about 15 times to form a smooth dough.

5. Form into 8 to 10 equal-size balls. Cover and let stand for 20 to 30 minutes.

6. Flatten dough, rolling away from you with a small wooden dowel or rolling pin, turning dough 1/8 turn after each roll. Tortillas should be about 5 inches in diameter and of a uniform thickness.

7. Cook tortillas on a preheated 350-degree comal, griddle, or skillet for 15 to 20 seconds on the first side; flip over and cook for 20 seconds more while pressing down with a spatula. Keep warm in a cloth towel.

# APPLE PIE TACOS

Dessert tacos aren't a traditional Mexican dish; however, we wanted to include one of our favorite creations. We decided on the simple approach in keeping with the easygoing and casual nature of tacos. Easy to prepare, these look like tacos and have the universally satisfying flavor of Mom's apple pie.

*Yield: 8 servings*

## Taco Filling
4 tart apples, peeled, cored, and cut in quarter-inch-thick slices
Dash salt
1/4 cup + 2 tablespoons granulated sugar
2 tablespoons all-purpose flour
2 teaspoons cornstarch
2 tablespoons butter

2 teaspoons ground Mexican canela or cinnamon
1/2 teaspoon ground allspice
1/2 cup apple juice

## Tacos
8 six-inch or 4 ten-inch flour tortillas, cut in half
2 to 3 tablespoons butter
1/8 cup powdered sugar
1 teaspoon ground Mexican canela or cinnamon

1. Preheat a heavy skillet or saucepan to medium (300 to 325 degrees).

2. Toss sliced apples with salt and 2 tablespoons of sugar, then with flour and cornstarch.

3. Place 2 tablespoons of butter in pan; when it sizzles, add apple slices.

4. Cook three to four minutes, stirring occasionally, until flour mixture combines with butter.

5. Add canela and allspice, then apple juice and 1/4 cup granulated sugar.

6. Bring to a slow boil and cook for 5 minutes, until apple slices are soft and sauce is smooth and thick. Allow to cool for a few minutes before using.

7. Spoon about 2 tablespoons of mixture on each tortilla and fold in half.

8. Melt some of the butter on a preheated comal, non-stick skillet, or griddle; place a filled tortilla in the butter. Cook about 1-1/2 minutes per side, until golden brown. Repeat for remaining tortillas. Caution: If the temperature is too high, the tortillas will brown before filling is heated through.

9. Dust tacos with powdered sugar and canela or cinnamon.

*Note: These may be prepared ahead of time and re-heated in a 325-degree oven.*

*Serving suggestion: Accompany tacos with vanilla or cinnamon ice cream, fruit sorbet, or whipped cream.*

# FRIJOLES CHARROS

*Yield: 8 servings*

6 ounces uncooked Mexican chorizo or hot Italian
    sausage, casings removed, then crumbled
2 slices smoked bacon, diced
1 medium white onion, chopped
2 cloves garlic, crushed
1 teaspoon toasted dried Mexican oregano
1/2 teaspoon toasted ground cumin seed
1 ancho chile, toasted, stemmed, and seeded, then crumbled
2 bay leaves
1 teaspoon pureed chipotle chile in adobo
1/2 teaspoon salt
3-1/2 cups cooked pinto beans
1 teaspoon apple cider vinegar
1-1/2 cups chicken or pork broth

1. Cook chorizo and bacon over medium heat until fat is rendered.
   Pour off half the fat.

2. Continue cooking and add onion and garlic. Cook until translucent,
   then add oregano, cumin, ancho chile, bay leaves, and chipotle.

3. Add salt, beans, vinegar, and stock. Simmer on low for 45
   minutes to 1 hour.

# SPICY COLESLAW

*Yield: 6 servings, enough to garnish 18 to 24 tacos*

3 tablespoons apple cider vinegar
1 tablespoon vegetable oil
1/4 cup freshly squeezed lime juice
1/8 cup honey
1 teaspoon salt
1/2 cup chopped fresh cilantro
1 head red or green cabbage, shredded (about
    1-1/2 pounds)
3 scallions, thinly sliced on the diagonal
2 to 3 jalapeño chiles, stemmed, seeded, and cut into
    very thin strips
1 large carrot, peeled and shredded

1. In a large bowl, combine liquids, salt, and cilantro with a whisk.

2. Toss with the remaining ingredients to evenly coat with the dressing.

3. Let the mixture stand at room temperature for at least 30 minutes;
   toss often before serving. For maximum color and flavor, serve
   within 3 to 4 hours.

# GUACAMOLE

*Yield: 6 servings*

**1 medium red onion**

**4 medium ripe Hass avocados**

**1 clove garlic, minced**

**2 to 3 serrano or jalapeño chiles, stemmed, seeded, and minced**

**1/2 cup chopped fresh cilantro**

**1/4 teaspoon ground cumin (optional)**

**Salt and pepper to taste**

**Juice of 1/2 lime**

1. Peel and cut onion in small dice. Rinse under hot water for 30 seconds, then in cold water for 30 seconds to remove the raw taste.

2. Peel and remove the pit from the avocados and place in a bowl or molcajete with all ingredients except salt, pepper, and lime.

3. Mash with hands, fork, or potato masher until avocado is fairly smooth and other ingredients have been well combined.

4. Adjust seasoning with salt and pepper.

5. Stir in lime juice when serving.

6. Garnish with Salsa Fresca (see p. 90) and/or grated, sharp aged cheese such as ricotta salata, cotija, or dry Monterey jack.

*Note: Guacamole will discolor when exposed to air. Take special care when storing to ensure it is well wrapped.*

# SALSA FRESCA

*Yield: about 3 cups*

**4 to 5 plum tomatoes, diced**
**1/2 teaspoon minced garlic**
**1/2 cup finely chopped red or white onion, rinsed under**
**    hot tap water for 30 seconds and under cold water**
**    for 30 more seconds, then drained**
**1/8 cup fresh lime juice**
**2 tablespoons mild vinegar such as apple cider vinegar or**
**    rice wine vinegar**
**2 or 3 fresh jalapeños, seeded and finely chopped**
**1/4 cup coarsely chopped cilantro**
**1 tablespoon olive oil (optional)**
**Salt to taste**

1. Put tomatoes, garlic, onion, lime juice, vinegar, jalapeños, and cilantro in a bowl and mix well. Mixture may be coarsely pureed in a food processor or left intact for more texture.

2. Add olive oil, if desired, and salt to taste. Let mixture sit for 30 minutes to allow flavors to develop.

# SALSA VERDE

*Yield: about 2 cups*

**1 dozen tomatillos, husked and rinsed under hot water**
**    to remove the sticky coating**
**6 garlic cloves, peeled**
**3 to 4 serrano chiles, stems removed,**
**    or use jalapeño chiles for a milder salsa**
**1 small white onion, finely chopped**
**Juice of 1/2 lime**
**1/2 teaspoon sugar**
**Salt to taste**
**1 bunch fresh cilantro**

1. Boil tomatillos in enough water to cover, along with half the garlic, half the chiles, and half the onion for about 10 minutes. Remove from heat and drain; reserve cooking water. Cool. Finely mince remaining garlic and chiles. Coarsely chop cilantro leaves.

2. Place tomatillos, cooked onions, garlic, and chiles in a blender or food processor and blend, adding a little of the cooking water if necessary. The sauce should be thick. Pour sauce into a bowl; stir in reserved garlic, chiles, remaining onion, cilantro, lime juice, and sugar; season with salt to taste.

# RESOURCES

**Dean & Deluca**
1. Catalog Department
(800) 221-7714
Web site: www.deandeluca.com
— *Dried chiles, dried posole, spices, hot sauces.*

2. 560 Broadway
New York, NY 10012
(212) 226-6800

3. 3276 M Street NW
Washington, DC 20007
(202) 342-2500

**El Paso Chile Company**
909 Texas Avenue
El Paso, TX 79901
(800) 274-7468
Web site: www.elpasochile.com
— *Bottled sauces, dips, pestos, etc.*

**Kalustyan's**
123 Lexington Avenue
   (between 28th & 29th)
New York, NY 10016
(212) 685-3451
Web site: www.kalustyans.com
— *Asian, Indian, and Mexican spices; nuts, dried fruit, grains, beans, and chile powders.*

**Mo Hotta Mo Betta**
(mail order only)
P.O. Box 4136
San Luis Obispo, CA 93406
(800) 462-3220
Web site: www.mohotta.com
— *Dried chiles, herbs, spices, hot sauces, and salsa.*

**Pendery's, Inc.**
1221 Manufacturing Street
Dallas, TX 75207
(800) 533-1870
(214) 741-1870
Web site: www.penderys.com
— *Dried chiles and spices.*

**Santa Fe School of Cooking**
116 West San Francisco Street
Santa Fe, NM 87501
(800) 982-4688
(505) 983-4511
(505) 983-7540 fax
Web site:
www.santafeschoolofcooking.com
— *Over twenty varieties of dried chiles and powders, chipotle chiles in adobo, herbs, spices, posole, Mexican chocolate, and more.*

# ⚙ ACKNOWLEDGMENTS ⚙

We would like to express our appreciation to past and present chefs of The Santa Fe School of Cooking for contributing their recipes and ideas. Past chefs include Janet Mitchell, Allen Smith, David Jones, Bill Weiland, Zach Calkins, and Peter Zimmer. We are most indebted to the staff at the school for all of their support including tasting, input, and proofreading.

A very special thanks to photographer Lois Ellen Frank and to her wonderful assistant, Walter Whitewater, for not only producing such great photographs but also for making food photography such a fun experience. We thank Lois for the use of her studio, kitchen, props, creativity, and especially for her patience. Thanks to Walter for his talented food styling.

There are too many taste testers to list all, but special acknowledgments to Cheryl Alters Jamison, Lois Stouffer, and Ellen Stelling. Marcia Jarrett provided kitchen assistance beyond the call of friendship.

# ☙ RESOURCES ☙

Noe Cano, sous chef at The Santa Fe School of Cooking, was invaluable in the food-styling and recipe-testing stages. Without Noe, this book would have been more difficult and a lot less fun. Thanks to Susan Thomas and Nicole Curtis for proofreading and tasting. Thanks also to all the chefs, staff, friends, and visitors of the school for their help and feedback during recipe testing.

We would like to express our appreciation to the following individuals and businesses for their contribution to this book: Fernando Olea Caballero of Bert's Taqueria for the use of his comal and for the wonderful taco feast he prepared; David Cohen of Old Mexico Grill for recipes, ideas, and a delicious taco lunch.

# ❧ INDEX ❧

# ⚘ SANTA FE SCHOOL OF COOKING AND MARKET ⚘

The Santa Fe School of Cooking is a regional cooking school that opened its doors in December 1989. Since its opening, thousands of guests have enjoyed taking classes, participating in culinary tours, and becoming part of the school's family. The adjacent market specializes in local products and has its own product line. A mail-order catalog is also available.

If you would like to receive information about the Santa Fe School of Cooking, please copy and fill out this form, then mail to the following address:

The Santa Fe School of Cooking
116 West San Francisco Street
Santa Fe, NM 87501
(800) 982-4688 catalog information
(505) 983-4511 class information
(505) 983-7540 fax

Check out our Web site for a current class schedule, information about special events, or shopping on-line: www.santafeschoolofcooking.com

Name _____

Address _____

City _____ State _____ Zip Code _____

Phone _____